W
Men and Women
Can't Be Friends

Honest Relationship Advice for Women

by Oliver Markus Malloy

Becker and Malloy
www.BeckerandMalloy.com

Ladies,

I have bad news for you. Men are pigs. No really. I know you think you know what I'm talking about but you don't know the half of it. You have no idea how depraved we men really are.

I'm about to tell you the truth about men. The whole truth. Not that sanitized holier-than-thou shit they feed you in all those other relationship books.

I'm gonna take you into the abyss that is the male mind. It's a dark and scary place. You're not gonna like it. It's dirty in there. Icky. Don't touch anything. Bring hand sanitizer.

Oliver

Table of Contents

YOU KNOW NOTHING ABOUT MEN

You probably think you know all about men, because you read a lot of romance novels, so you think you're an expert on men. But I'm gonna tell you a little secret: the men in those books are fiction. They do not at all represent how men in real life actually think. Those romance novels were written for women by women (and a few men who know what women like to read, so they write romance to make a quick buck.)

When you read a book like Grey, Christian's inner monologue does not at all sound like how a man actually thinks in real life. It sounds like a woman does a poor job of imagining how a man thinks. The fictitious men in romance novels are as fake and imaginary as vampires. They're not real.

Right about now, there's probably a little voice in your head, screaming: "NOOO!!! You can't say that! You can't speak for all men! Every man is different!!"

True. No two dogs are alike. And yet, all dogs have something in common that makes them dogs, and makes them different from cats. The same goes for men and women. The trouble starts when cats don't realize that dogs are different. Dogs think differently, and perceive the world differently, than cats do. I'm a dog. You're a cat. And a dog knows better what it's like to be a dog than a cat does.

There's a reason why most men don't read romance: Romance novels are wish-fulfillment for women. The fictitious men in romance novels fall all over themselves trying to please a woman. Does that sound like your real life experience with men? No of course not. (Except for guys who want to fuck you. There is no man more attentive as the guy who wants to fuck you for the first time.)

That's why you read romance. To get something you don't get in real life. Because your husband's idea of romance is bringing out the trash and not farting during sex.

Men are not into romance. We only pretend to be into romance for the benefit of women. Romance is something we men do to woo women. Romance is hard work for us. To a man, reading about romance is not only totally unrealistic, but also boring. It's like reading about work. How thrilling would a book about ironing be to you? Now imagine if the heroine in the book was much better at ironing than you, and reading about her perfect ironing skills made you feel pretty inadequate by comparison. That, in a nutshell, is what it's like for a man to read about the super-romantic fictitious men in romance novels.

More than 90% of romance readers are women. It's a book genre entirely geared towards women, the same way Valentine's Day flowers are geared towards women. We men have as much interest in reading about romance as we have in receiving flowers. Close to zero.

So what are men really like? How do we really think?

THE MEANING OF LIFE

What is the meaning of life? Why are we here?

Philosophers have pondered that question for centuries. I'm afraid the answer is disappointingly simple: Mating.

That's it.

Christians seem to think that life is a test, and that the goal is to get into Heaven. But that's like saying your job is to get a promotion. No, your job is to work. And then, if you worked hard, then you get promoted. Heaven is supposed to be a reward or promotion, for a job well done. And what's our job? "Be fruitful and multiply." We are here to mate and procreate. That's it. That's all there's to it. That's the meaning of life. Mating.

What is the meaning of life for a virus? It's not to make people sick. That's just an unfortunate side effect of its life cycle. A virus exists for one single purpose: to replicate itself. And in the process, its host might get sick, because the virus is doing too good of a job of replicating itself.

We like to romanticize the wild, raw, majestic beauty of nature. But when you take a closer look, nature is really just a giant fuckfest. That beautiful bird chirping? It's a mating call. That pretty little bird is trying to get laid. And why does the peacock have such beautiful feathers? To attract females. Because he's trying to get laid.

Animals in the wild spend their entire lives trying to stay alive, and to mate. That's it. They eat, they sleep, they fuck, they raise their offspring. That's the meaning of their lives.

And as much as we like to pretend that we are civilized and that we are oh-so different from all those other animals, deep down we are really just like them. Mating has been programmed into our DNA. And that programming always influences our interaction with the opposite sex, whether we like to admit it or not.

It's normal to find someone else (typically the opposite sex) attractive. But what do we really mean when we use the word *attractive?* We mean *sexually* attractive. We mean that other person looks so yummy, they look like they would make a great mating partner.

What does the word *sexy* mean? It means we find someone sexually attractive, and we'd love to mate with them, even if we usually don't say that out loud in polite company. If you find Robert Downey Jr. sexy, can you honestly say you wouldn't want to have sex with him if the opportunity ever presented itself? No, you can't, because that's exactly what you mean when you say he's sexy.

That's why we all strive to be as attractive as possible. We are trying to attract as many potential mates as possible. We want to look desirable. We want others to want to mate with us. No different than a colorful peacock. When girls dress up for their night out at the club, they are doing what all animals do when they try to make themselves desirable for a potential mate. That's the whole point behind the fashion, perfume, cosmetics, diet, and plastic surgery industries.

The red lipstick? It's supposed to signal fertility and readiness to mate. Just like the swollen red butt of a baboon. That tight-fitting little dress that shows off your curves? From the standpoint of evolutionary biology, big breasts represent a healthy mate who can feed a lot of offspring. That's why we men are programmed to like big tits. When you show off your curves, what you're really doing is advertising to the whole world: "Look at me! I'm a healthy female! I'd be a perfect mate! Come mount me!"

When guys try to get a good job and make a lot of money, it's so that we can find a good mate, because we know women like guys with money. Big tits are to us men, what big wallets are to you womenfolk. A sexy woman can have almost any man she wants. And a rich guy can have almost any woman he wants.

Everything we men do, everything we men have done for the past 100,000 years, is all about attracting a mate. When a guy tries to impress a girl with his fancy car, or his expensive suit, or his gold watch, or his flashy shirt at the club, or he flexes his biceps, or brags about how much money he makes, he's doing the same thing that animals have done for millions of years. Like a peacock, he's trying to make himself desirable and to attract a mate.

And it all starts in childhood, long before we even think about sex. When little girls dream about being a princess, they want to meet a prince to live happily ever after... and mate with him, even when they don't quite understand the biological details of mating yet. When they fantasize about their dream wedding, they may not be thinking about intercourse yet, but they dream about finding the perfect mate.

MATING: EVERYONE'S DOING IT

Mating (and its many facets: sex, porn, romantic comedies, romance novels, dating tips, relationship advice, fashion, make-up tips, wedding planning, parenting advice, etc.) is such an all-important topic to us, we not only love to mate, we also love to even just think about it, read about it, and talk about it. Does even just one day go by where we don't think about mating somehow?

"What freedom men and women could have, were they not constantly tricked and trapped and enslaved and tortured by their sexuality! The only drawback in that freedom is that without it one would not be a human. One would be a monster."
(John Steinbeck)

We all know that sex is the most interesting topic in the world. We love to talk about sex. There's no juicier gossip than who is sleeping with whom. And we love to read about sex. Check the top 1000 books on Amazon. Most of them have a shirtless guy on the cover, because they're smutty "romance novels" (read: porn for women) about a girl being swept off her feet by one (or more) billionaire alpha-males. There are literally tens of thousands of books out there about shirtless billionaire alpha-male vampires who can't wait to mate with you. Lucky you! And women eat that shit up! Men, not so much. We men prefer to watch actual porn. And there's a perfectly good explanation for that. Men like to see naked skin and big tits. Women like to fantasize about big wallets. They find money erotic. Search for "billionaire romance" books on Amazon. There are 66,581 search results. And virtually all of these "money is sooo sexy, I want my very own billionaire!" books were written by women for women. Big surprise there.

"There are a number of mechanical devices which increase sexual arousal, particularly in women. Chief among these is the Mercedes-Benz 380SL convertible."
(P.J. O'Rourke)

Look at the huge success of Fifty Shades of Grey. The girl in the book lets a rich guy beat her and ritually rape her, and she likes it! She finds it erotic! But imagine if Christian Grey wasn't a billionaire. Imagine if he lived in a dirty old trailer down by the river. Then that story wouldn't be a sexy romance novel, but an episode of CSI.

Nowadays it's politically correct to pretend that men and women are equal. But we all know that we're not. Not better or worse, but men and women are definitely different. And they have been programmed to play different roles during the mating process. You women like to call us men pigs or dogs, because we always seem to want sex. And men call women gold diggers and money-hungry whores, because money seems so important to you.

During the cavemen days, a lot of you women died during child birth. Or you got eaten by a sabre tooth tiger, or died from an infection. In order to guarantee the survival of the species, we men were programmed to mate with as many different females as possible, and to spread our seed, since we never knew how many of you females actually survived the pregnancy and how many of those babies actually grew up. Impregnating just one single female, and putting all our eggs in one basket, would have been a risky gamble.

Meanwhile, those of you women who actually survived

pregnancy, you were programmed to raise your offspring. You were programmed to create a nest. A home for the child. That's not easy when you have to fend for yourself. Raising a kid is easier if you have help and support.

As a result, humans invented something called family. But it didn't look like the monogamous families we know today. Back then a family was one guy with many different women. That way we got to spread our seed, and even if a couple of you women died, our offspring still had a pretty good chance of survival. And you pregnant women helped each other raise your kids.

MARRIAGE: ONE MAN WITH MANY WIVES

Polygamist Mormons really aren't all that weird. Their idea of family is older than ours. For tens of thousands of years, family was never really about the romantic notion of love between a man and a woman as we are led to believe today. Family was about ensuring the survival of the species. The idea of marrying for love is a fairly new invention. Marriages used to be arranged, or forced. (Trigger warning: You're about to have your mind blooown. POOF!)

"For men, the underlying evolutionary calculus of polygamy is clear: the possibility for a larger number of offspring and thus enhanced evolutionary fitness. For women, the reasoning is more nuanced: the possibility of better genes for their children, improved access to material resources and social advancement. It can be argued that a woman would be better off as the 20th wife of a very wealthy man than as the only wife of a pauper."
(Time.com)

In the beginning, we men simply took whichever female we wanted, whether you liked it or not. And we men didn't ask you womanfolk for permission when we wanted to have sex with you. Bride kidnapping, also known as marriage by abduction or marriage by capture is a practice in which a man abducts the woman he wants to marry. Bride kidnapping was a normal thing to do all over the world all throughout history. And these kidnappings and ritualized rapes are still part of many cultures around the globe today.

"Until the 18th century, it was common practice for grooms to abduct brides before the wedding. Bride kidnapping has been a thing since the founding of Rome,

when Romulus threw a giant party, invited the people of Sabine to a party, and then stole all their women. English brides could expect to be kidnapped until the Marriage Act was passed in 1753, and mock-kidnappings are still a wedding tradition in parts of Eastern Europe. Sadly, the real thing is still practiced all over the world."
(BuzzFeed.com)

"Bride kidnapping is an ancient tradition of physically abducting your future wife. She may be a girl you have spotted and like the look of, though usually she is a complete stranger. While it may prove more convenient than dating in the long run, usually the girls put up quite a fight. In Petr Lom's documentary on bride kidnapping, you can watch a 25-year-old Norkuz be brought to her new home against her will, crying. The groom's female relatives hold her down, and try to force a wedding headscarf onto her head. If they succeed, then she is committed to stay otherwise she will bring shame on herself and her family. This is a common practice.
(Vice.com)

"They call it ala kachuu, or "grab and run." In Kyrgyzstan, as many as 40% of ethnic Kyrgyz women are married after being kidnapped by the men who become their husbands, according to a local NGO. Two-thirds of these bride kidnappings are non-consensual... Typically, a would-be groom gathers a group of young men, and together they drive around looking for a woman he wants to marry. The unsuspecting woman is often literally dragged off the street, bundled into the car and taken straight to the man's house - where frequently the family will have already started making preparations for the wedding."
(Newsweek)

"Bride kidnapping also exists in the oldest mythologies. According to the Bible's Book of Judges, the tribe of Benjamin slaughtered all the men and non-virgins from the neighboring town so they could kidnap and wed the virgins. They were instructed, "Go and hide in the vineyards. When the women of Shiloh come out for their dances, rush out from the vineyards, and each of you can take one of them home to be your wife!"
(Vice.com)

Yupp, you read that right. In the bible, rape was not only common practice, it was the right thing to do! (POOF! Mind blown!) Supposedly God told his followers to go kidnap and rape the women of neighboring tribes. According to the bible, God condoned and even encouraged rape. That right there is a pretty good indication that the bible was not written by a divine being, but written by a bunch of horny, misogynist men. That's just how we guys operate. It's no coincidence that there is no commandment that says "Thou shalt not rape."

"Rape is normative in the Jewish and Christian Scriptures. The texts in which women are raped are legion: Numbers 31:15-18; Deuteronomy 21:10-14; Judges 19:22-26. Shockingly, for many religious readers, God, Moses and the Torah call for the rape of women (and killing of their infants) as a normative practice in war. Dr. Kate Blanchard expresses the horror of the unsuspecting reader:

"Quick -- which famous religious personality voiced this angry tirade: "Remove your veil, take off the skirt, uncover the thigh... Your nakedness shall be uncovered, your shame will be seen; I will take vengeance"? Or this: "It is for the

greatness of your iniquity that your skirts are lifted up, and you suffer violence... I myself will lift up your skirts over your face, and your shame will be seen"? Or this: "She did not give up her whorings... in her youth men had lain with her and fondled her virgin bosom and poured out their lust upon her. Therefore I delivered her into the hands of her lovers, for whom she lusted. They uncovered her nakedness... and they killed her with the sword. Judgment was executed upon her, and she became a byword among women"?

Yep, you guessed it: The God of the Hebrew and Christian scriptures (Isaiah 47, Jeremiah 13, and Ezekiel 23). The translations of these shining examples of victim-blaming are clear enough, despite the old-fashioned language: I'm angry and you're going to suffer for it. You deserve to be raped because of your sexual exploits. You're a slut and it was just a matter of time till you suffered the consequences. Let this be a lesson to you and to all other uppity women."
Dr. Blanchard's blog, "Rape is God's Problem Too," points to the ways assumptions about the right of males (human and divine) to do whatever they want to the bodies of human women -- no feminine divines here -- especially in the name of "love," is deeply embedded in our civil and religious cultures."
(Huffington Post)

Some say that the honeymoon is a relic of marriage by capture. The husband went into hiding with his kidnapped wife to avoid reprisals from her relatives, and tried to get her pregnant by the end of the month. (POOF!)

Throughout history, powerful males simply took lots of females. The more the merrier. Charlemagne was a great conqueror who united Europe under his rule. And he had sex with so many of you women that virtually every European today can trace their ancestry back to him. (POOF!)

Genghis Khan was another one of those fuckmeisters. He was the great-great-great-grandpa of millions of people today, because he had sex with so many women during his conquests. He did an excellent job spreading his seed. Genghis Khan is estimated to be a direct ancestor for 8 percent of the population of Central Asia today. (POOF!)

That's just the way it was back then. Powerful men had harems full of fertile young women. And when we conquered another tribe, we stole and raped the other tribe's women. Nobody could stop us, so we did whatever we wanted. Men like Charlemagne and Genghis Khan are examples of what we men would do with you women if we could still do whatever we want. (I know, right? Sick!)

MONOGAMY: THE NEW KID ON THE BLOCK

Only about 3 percent of animal species are monogamous. A couple of penguins, some otters and a few other oddball critters. To these select few it comes natural to mate for life and never look at another member of the opposite sex. We humans are not part of that little club. Like the other 97% of species, we humans are not monogamous by nature. We just pretend that we are.

"Face it: Monogamy is unnatural

Biologically, we humans are animals. So it makes sense to look to the animal kingdom for clues as to what we are built for.

The evidence shows that monogamy is a rarity among mammals. Only 3% to 5% of all the mammal species on Earth "practice any form of monogamy." In fact, no mammal species has been proven to be truly monogamous.

As recent as over 100 years ago, it was far more likely that an individual would lose his or her spouse at a young age. Remarriage by widows and widowers - also known as serial monogamy - was one way for humans to fulfill the need for sexual variety.

Human monogamy is influenced by many factors. Instead of pointing fingers or acting morally superior toward those who stray from marriages, we should recognize that strict sexual fidelity is a lofty but perhaps fundamentally doomed aspiration."
(CNN.com)

DOING IT LIKE MAMMALS
ON THE DISCOVERY CHANNEL

Monogamy is a fairly recent human invention. Prior to that, we men spread our seed the same way most animals do. Have you ever noticed that the mating scenes in nature documentaries look a little bit like the male is raping the female? That's because he is. In nature there is really no difference between mating and raping. It's pretty much one and the same thing.

Here's what the smart folks at Yale University have to say about rape in nature:

"The evidence suggests that natural selection, which has equipped men with a psychological apparatus designed to maximize the total number of female copulations, may lead them to rape as a byproduct of this tendency or, frighteningly, because in certain environmental conditions, rape is a behavior that enhances reproductive success.

Perhaps the most informative insight into rape, however, comes from the meticulous work of zoologists and animal behaviorists. In non-human species, it is possible to study the incidence and significance of rape after taking culture out of the equation. Indeed, rape is common in the animal kingdom, and is observed in insects, 39 species of birds, reptiles, fish, marine mammals and the great apes. Some organisms, like the scorpionfly and the waterstrider, have evolved specific appendages for committing rape.

Similarly, our close evolutionary relatives, the orangutans, consist of dominant and subordinate males, and the subordinates reproduce by raping unguarded females. It is estimated that between one-third and one-half of orangutan copulations are rapes.

In the vast majority of the animal world - our world - rape occurs with regularity in the absence of cultural factors.

The upshot of this discussion is that most of what we are taught about the causes of rape is wrong. Many men and other animals are very prone to rape females if they feel that there is little cost for doing so, and that it is highly unlikely that this biological tendency can be trained out of people."
(Yale Daily News)

We men have always wanted to have sex with as many of you fertile young women as possible. It's part of a man's basic programming. That hasn't changed. Civilization is nothing more than an artificial and very thin veneer hiding our deep-seated primitive urges. The only reason why we men don't rape women all day long today, is because nowadays we have laws against that sort of thing, and we're afraid we'll get in trouble.

And then there are those really powerful men, who don't fear getting in trouble, so they, like Charlemagne and Genghis Khan, do whatever they want. Know what I mean?

#metoo

THE UGLY TRUTH

Whenever law and order breaks down, things get rapey real quick. In World War 2, there was a famous incident when Japanese soldiers conquered the Chinese city of Nanking, and raped everything that moved:

(Triggerrrrr Warninggggg! If you're a Nancy, you better close your eyes for the next 2 or 3 pages. It's not pretty. This chapter is pretty shocking actually.)

"In what became known as the "Rape of Nanking," the Japanese butchered an estimated 150,000 male "war prisoners," massacred an additional 50,000 male civilians, and raped at least 20,000 women and girls of all ages, many of whom were mutilated or killed in the process." (History.com)

Japanese soldiers systematically went from door to door, searching for girls. They captured all the females they could find and gang-raped them. The women were often killed immediately after being raped. The soldiers mutilated them or penetrated their vaginas with bayonets, long sticks of bamboo, or other objects. They did not even spare young children.

But the raping of Nanking was by no means an isolated incident. That sort of thing happens every time men feel like they can get away with it without getting in trouble for it.

"From the systematic rape of women in Bosnia, to an estimated 200,000 women raped during the battle for Bangladeshi independence in 1971, to Japanese rapes

during the 1937 occupation of Nanking - the past century offers too many examples."
(BBC News)

"Rape in war is as old as war itself. After the sack of Rome 16 centuries ago Saint Augustine called rape in wartime an "ancient and customary evil". For soldiers, it has long been considered one of the spoils of war."
(The Economist)

"South Sudan Allowed Troops to Rape and Loot Instead of Paying Them
A new report from the UN human rights office is accusing the US-backed government of South Sudan of a series of horrific war crimes in their ongoing civil war, saying it has created one of the "most horrendous human rights situations in the world." Officials say that the South Sudanese government encouraged troops and their militia allies to loot private property and rape women as a way of getting out of paying them, with the UN saying they documented 1,300 rapes in Unity State alone over the course of six months."
(Antiwar.com)

"U.S. military men sexually assault one-third of fellow female soldiers
In July, CNN reported on a House committee hearing on sexual abuse within the military. Forty-one percent of female veterans at an L.A. veteran's hospital reported male soldiers had sexually assaulted them, and 29 percent were raped, said Rep. Jane Harman (D-Cali.) to the committee. "We have an epidemic here," Harman said. "Women serving in the U.S. military today are more likely to be raped by a fellow soldier than killed by enemy fire in Iraq."

"More than 20,000 Muslim girls and women have been raped in Bosnia since fighting began in April 1992, according to a European Community fact-finding team. Teenage girls have been a particular target in Bosnia and Herzegovina and Croatia, according to The State of the World's Children 1996 report.

In some raids in Rwanda, virtually every adolescent girl who survived an attack by the militia was subsequently raped.

The State of the World's Children 1996 report notes that the disintegration of families in times of war leaves women and girls especially vulnerable to violence. Nearly 80 per cent of the 53 million people uprooted by wars today are women and children. When fathers, husbands, brothers and sons are drawn away to fight, they leave women, the very young and the elderly to fend for themselves. In Bosnia and Herzegovina, Myanmar and Somalia, refugee families frequently cite rape or the fear of rape as a key factor in their decisions to seek refuge.

Sexual assault presents a major problem in camps for refugees and the displaced, according to the report. The incidence of rape was reported to be alarmingly high at camps for Somali refugees in Kenya in 1993. The camps were located in isolated areas, and hundreds of women were raped in night raids or while foraging for firewood."
(Unicef)

"ISIS tells fighters to gang rape women saying sex with multiple jihadis makes them muslim

It emerged as victims of the perverted hate group spoke out about its infamous sex slave markets, where twisted militants can buy women for as little as a packet of cigarettes. ISIS fighters have previously executed women who refused to have sex with them, with many experts saying most young men joining the group are more interested in sex than Islam or jihad."
(Express.co.uk)

The instinct to mate with every woman they can get their hands on is part of man's nature. Just like a dog, who will hump just about anything, including your leg. Has your dog ever asked for your permission before humping your leg? Nope. Your dog is a furry little rapist. Law and order, and a man-made invention called civilization, are the only things stopping men from doing to women what we have done for tens of thousands of years.

"More than 100 women and girls have come forward with reports of sexual assault and robbery by gangs of men in the German city of Cologne on New Year's Eve 2015.

Victims have described chaos outside the city's main train station, as the men carried out dozens of attacks with little apparent response from the authorities.

Some of the women caught in the violence have begun speaking of their ordeal. Michelle told the BBC News how she and her friends became surrounded by between 20 and 30 men, who were speaking a foreign language. "They grabbed our arms... pushed our clothes away, and tried to get between our legs or I don't know where."

One woman, whose identity has been protected, told

German television how gangs of men assaulted her in the crowd. "All of a sudden these men around us began groping us," she said. "They touched our behinds and grabbed between our legs. They touched us everywhere."

One victim, named as Busra, spoke of a sense of lawlessness outside the station, where the attackers felt they could do as they pleased. "They felt like they were in power and that they could do anything with the women who were out in the street partying," she said. "They touched us everywhere. It was truly terrible."
(BBC News)

And this stuff doesn't just happen in other countries or in war zones. Rape is shockingly common in America:

"Sexual violence (SV) is a significant problem in the United States. SV refers to sexual activity where consent is not obtained or not given freely. Anyone can experience SV, but most victims are female. The person responsible for the violence is typically male and usually someone known to the victim. The person can be, but is not limited to, a friend, coworker, neighbor, or family member."
(Centers for Disease Control and Prevention)

According to the CDC, one in five women in America have been raped. 51.1% of them were raped by their intimate partner. 40.8% were raped by an aquaintance.

"One in four college women have survived either rape or attempted rape in their lifetime. The US Department of Justice published a study in 2006 of over 4,000 college women. In that survey, 3% of those women had survived rape or attempted rape in a 7 month academic year, alone.

An additional 21% had survived rape or attempted rape at some point in their lives prior to that academic year. When you take those two figures and add them up - the 3 and the 21 - you get 24%, or roughly one in four."
(Findings from the national violence against women survey. Research in Brief, Washington, DC: National Institute of Justice, US Department of Justice.)

Take a moment to ponder this statistical fact:

98% of rapists are men.
(RAINN: Rape, Abuse and Incest National Network)

In other words, almost 100% of rapists are men, and almost 0% of rapists are women. That should tell you one very important fact:

Men and women are not equal when it comes to sex. There is a very big difference between the sex drive in us men, and the sex drive in you women.

"Desire is in men a hunger, in women only an appetite."
(Mignon McLaughlin)

We men really, really, *really* like sex. We like sex so much, many of us are willing to risk getting in serious trouble to get it. That's why laws against rape haven't stopped rape, and why laws against prostitution haven't stopped prostitution, and why men who cheat on their wives would continue to cheat even if it was illegal, and why gay men continue to be gay even in fundamentalist religious countries like Saudi Arabia, where homosexuality is punishable by death.

And it's the reason why all these high powered sex scandals you hear about on the news really aren't surprising. Disgusting and disturbing, yes, but not surprising. Men have abused their power over women for tens of thousands of years. The surprising thing is not that it's still happening. The surprising thing is that it's not happening more often.

IT'S ALWAYS ABOUT SEX. ALWAYS.

We men supposedly think about sex every few seconds. Maybe that's a bit of an exaggeration. But it's true that we men think about sex a lot throughout the day. Probably more than about any other topic.

"A student undergoing a word-association test was asked why a snowstorm put him in mind of sex. He replied frankly: 'because everything does.'"
(Honor Tracy)

And when we men think about sex, we do not only think about having sex with one woman, but preferably with lots and lots of you women. Every man has dreamed about a threesome at some point or another. Or even an orgy, with him starring in the leading role. It's just part of being a man.

If there were no negative consequences to consider, if there was no jail sentence, no angry wife, and no expensive divorce lawyers, then a man would try to have sex with every attractive female who crosses his path. It's probably not easy for a woman like you to understand what it's like to be a man. Imagine you're starving, and someone puts a huge buffet in front of you. There's delicious, mouth-watering food all around you, and it's really really hard not to eat it all. That's what it's like to be a man around attractive women. The urge to want to hump everything that moves is part of a man's natural programming. It's a deep-seated hunger. To suppress that hunger takes civilization and a lot of willpower.

"You want an inconvenient truth? Try this one: human

beings are clearly evolved for sex lives featuring multiple simultaneous sexual relationships. Men, especially, are designed by evolution to be attracted to sexual novelty and to gradually lose sexual attraction to the same partner in the absence of such novelty. The so-called Coolidge Effect is well demonstrated in social mammals of all sorts, and is old news to anyone knowledgeable about reproductive biology. Boys will be boys, and men will be the way they are, despite the many ways our society tries to make them change."
(PsychologyToday.com)

Studies have shown that smart men tend to be better at suppressing their primitive urges than dumb men. Well-educated men value their relationships more, because they understand the many benefits a stable long-term relationship brings with it. Life is easier when you face it together with a team mate. Meanwhile, uneducated knuckle-draggers, who have nothing, and have no prospects for the future, are quicker to sleep around, because the instant gratification of having sex with yet another baby mama is more important to them than the damaging long term consequences of destroying their relationship.

"Intelligent men are less likely to cheat on their wives because of evolution, a new analysis of social trends indicates.

Researchers at a British university found that men with higher IQs place greater value on monogamy and sexual exclusivity than their less intelligent peers.

The patterns were uncovered by Dr Satoshi Kanazawa of the London School of Economics and Political Science in a paper published in the March edition of the journal Social Psychology Quarterly.

He concluded: "As the empirical analysis shows, more intelligent men are more likely to value monogamy and sexual exclusivity than less intelligent men."

Dr Kanazawa claims that the correlation between intelligence and monogamy in men has its origins in evolutionary development. Sexual exclusivity is an "evolutionary novel" quality that would have been of little benefit to early man, who was programmed to be promiscuous, he argues.

The modern world no longer confers such an evolutionary advantage to men who have several sexual partners - but only intelligent men are able to shed the psychological baggage of their species and adopt new modes of behaviour. Other "evolutionary novel" qualities that are more common among people of higher intelligence include liberalism and atheism, his study indicated."
(Telegraph.co.uk)

But even the smartest among us men do dumb things. When a successful family father cheats on his wife, the rational part of his brain knows that it might destroy his family and he might lose his wife, his kids and his home. And yet, he risks it all and fucks his secretary anyway. Why? Because he just couldn't help himself. The rational, civilized part of his brain failed to suppress the primitive impulse to mate with as many different women as possible.

WHY DO MEN CHEAT?

We have all seen the tabloid news about some famous actor who has a really hot wife or girlfriend, and then gets caught cheating on her with some other woman who doesn't even look half as good as the one he has at home. Why? Was it because the other woman knew some amazing trick and sex with her was so much better than with his wife? Probably not.

Did he and his wife have marital problems and he just connected with that other woman on a deeper emotional level? Maybe. But the most likely answer is that he fucked her simply because she was someone else, and not his wife. His urge was not to fuck someone better than his wife, but to fuck someone more. More than one. The more the better.

And that's why we men like to watch porn. Even the men who are civilized enough to keep our dick in our pants, and our urges under control, and who do not cheat on our wives, still like to look at other women naked and fantasize about having sex with them.

Not because he doesn't love his wife, or he's not happy with her. But simply because he has that ancient urge to mate with more women than one. And watching porn gives him that outlet. At least in his head. And if your man says he doesn't like to watch porn, he's lying, because he's afraid of losing you.

"Research Suggests All Men Watch Pornography
Researchers at the University of Montreal were unable to carry out a study comparing the views of men who had never watched porn with those of regular users because

they were unable to find a single man who hadn't seen it!
"We started our research seeking men in their 20s who had never consumed pornography," said Professor Simon Louis Lajeunesse. "We couldn't find any."
(Huffington Post)

If your husband admits to you that he watches porn, don't make him feel guilty. He can't help being attracted to the female form. It's just part of being a man.

And don't feel threatened. Don't worry that he's not happy with you or the way you look. That's not why he's watching porn. You could be the most beautiful woman in the world, and he'd still be curious to see as many other women naked as possible. It doesn't mean he doesn't love or appreciate you. And it doesn't mean he wants to leave you for a sexier woman.

Why do you like to read romance novels? Should your husband feel threatened that you like to fantasize about billionaire alpha-males? The same age-old mating instinct that drives a man to want to see as many naked women as possible, drives women to want to fantasize about a guy with as much money as possible. The only difference between the two is that they appeal to the different roles men and women play during the mating process. We men want to spread our seed, and you women want to build a comfortable, stable nest for your offspring. Porn satisfies that urge in a man the same way a billionaire romance novel satisfies that urge in a woman. It scratches an itch.

FEMINISM

Of course that doesn't mean that we men don't like money, or that you women don't like sex. But the priorities tend to be different. I think there's something to the old saying that you women use sex to get love, and we men use love to get sex. And love is really just a word we use to describe a close bond, or relationship, between two people. We men have been programmed to want sex, so we do whatever is necessary to be in a relationship with a woman. And you women are programmed to want the stability and (financial) security of a relationship, so she offers the man what he wants: sex.

That symbiosis has worked pretty well for tens of thousands of years. You women stayed home and raised your offspring, while we men were out, hunting and gathering, or plundering and pillaging, or selling insurance at our shitty 9-5 jobs.

And then something weird happened: In the 20th century, you women suddenly got all uppedy and demanded equal rights. Being a man's sperm receptacle just wasn't enough for you anymore all of a sudden. Go figure. You wanted to vote, be heard, be respected as equals, and have the same opportunities as men. You no longer wanted to be treated as a man's property, or a man's sex slave.

"Marriage is for woman the commonest mode of livelihood, and the total amount of undesired sex endured by women is probably greater in marriage than in prostitution."
(Bertrand Russell)

Suddenly you women wanted to be able to go to work and earn your own living. You wanted to be able to support yourselves, without the need for a man. Feminism and the equal rights movement were born. A lot of us men were pretty scared by this new idea that you didn't need us anymore.

When women entered the work force in droves, society changed. Up until this pretty recent point in human history, men and women didn't really mingle all that much. You women stayed to yourselves, and we men stayed to ourselves. Men and women really only interacted when it came to mating. Other than that, we men locked our women away to make sure no other man could mate with them. That's why to this day women in the Middle East wear burkas.

When conservative men proclaimed that they would never allow their wives to work, it was only partly hurt pride and the desire to be the sole breadwinner of the family. Another part was fear. Fear of letting our wives interact with other men, and possibly liking some other man better, and running off with him.

The 20th century saw a dramatic increase in you women joining a male-dominated work force and being able to ensure your own survival without the need for a man. That was good. (But also pretty scary for many men.)

But there was also a flip side to that: since all of a sudden so many more men and women interacted with each other at work every day, the number of affairs, and broken marriages, increased dramatically. How could it not? If a woman spends 8 hours in an office with some other man, and only about 3 or 4 hours after work with her husband at home, it's no surprise if she ends up having more things in common with the guy at work, and the marriage falls apart.

It's politically incorrect to point out that the number of divorces sky-rocketed since you women joined the work force. But it's true. Whether that's a good or a bad thing depends on how you look at marriage. If you consider the marriage between a man and a woman to be the only right way to raise offspring, then all these divorces are obviously a bad thing.

But if you look at marriage for what it has traditionally been for thousands of years, an arrangement in which women were subservient to men and your survival depended on the whim of the man, then maybe it's not so bad that traditional marriage is slowly being phased out, just like we phased out rape and kidnapping at some point, and we phased out polygamy.

"The feminist movement contributed to the growing trend of divorce in the United States during the 1970's. There were a variety of ways in which feminists either subtly or overtly, encouraged divorce. Their success in liberalizing divorce laws to provide options for unhappy or abused women was one such way. The feminist argument that marriage was a form of oppression, as marriage meant sex-role segregation also led to the pursuit of divorce. Next, equal pay and access to high paying jobs, the results of tireless efforts of the feminists, allowed women to become economically independent. This meant that marriage wasn't necessary for financial stability any longer, and economic dependence had been one reason so many unhappy women stayed in marriages."

Nowadays it has become much easier for a female to meet many different men throughout your life. And we men are exposed to far more attractive females throughout our day than ever before in history. That is obviously not a good thing for traditional marriage. Today, temptation is everywhere. And because we men are programmed to have sex with as many women as possible, it takes a lot of willpower not to give in to that instinct and remain faithful.

STRUGGLING TO BE MONOGAMOUS

Being faithful and monogamous is not natural for human beings. It takes work. Deep down we all know that. We have all been tempted to stray at some point or another. Even when it was only a fleeting thought and we didn't act on it. Every time we acknowledge that someone of the opposite sex is "attractive" or "sexy" we are doing nothing other than pointing out that they would be a suitable mate. Not acting on that natural impulse to want to mate with a viable mating partner requires a conscious decision. It's a constant struggle between what your body wants, and what the civilized part of your brain says you should do, in order to avoid the negative consequences of cheating on your spouse and ruining your long-term relationship. That's why affairs, and extra-marital sex, are often referred to as "a moment of weakness."

Envy is the desire to have what someone else has. Jealousy is the fear of losing what you have. The more insecure you are about yourself or your relationship, the more jealous you are, because you are afraid to lose your significant other to someone else. That's why you women get jealous when we men interact with attractive females. Hiring an ugly babysitter or secretary? No problem. No threat. Hiring a sexy babysitter/secretary? Oh hell no!

The sexier the other woman is, the more jealous our wife gets. And that's where slut shaming comes from. When a woman is too sexually attractive, when she's too good at attracting the attention of the opposite sex, other women will shame her for it, because you are afraid she will steal your man.

And we all know that even though work relationships are frowned upon in the corporate world, the truth is, they happen all the time. When people spend most of their time at work, and most of their interactions with other human beings take place at work, of course it's only natural that this environment is where people meet potential mates. It's no different than high school or college in that regard. If you work at an office where there is not a lot of options, it may not happen for you, and you have to look for a mate in a club or online. But if you work with a lot of people of the opposite sex, you are bound to run into a viable mate at some point. That's why kids in high school and college hook up with each other all the time.

Even if you're already in a serious relationship, and you have no intention of jeopardizing that relationship, you may unintentionally do things that lead to problems down the road. It's a slippery slope: That guy at work is so nice. He's a great friend. He's so helpful. He always holds the door open for you. Always helps you when the copier is jammed. Always sits with you at lunch. Always has some interesting chit chat or a funny joke. But as long as you don't actually have sex with him, it's ok, right? No, it's not ok. But he's just a friend! Yeah, but his friendliness has an ulterior motive. That friendly behavior is how we males pursue you females these days, since raping and kidnapping are frowned upon nowadays.

Don't believe me that the only reason why that guy is so friendly and helpful to you is because he's trying to get in your pants? Do a quick Google search for the term "if it wasn't for sex" and you will get 129,000,000 search results that show you how we men really feel about interacting with women. You'll get millions of results like these:

If it wasn't for sex, men would not cater to women.

If it wasn't for sex, men would avoid women like the plague.

If it wasn't for sex, men wouldn't even talk to women.

JUST FRIENDS?

Researchers have done some serious studies on the question of whether men and women can be "just friends." The conclusion? No, we can't. Our ancient biological programming is just too strong. When we interact with the opposite sex, we always fall back into primitive mating behavior at some point or another. Harmless flirting? Not so harmless.

"Researchers asked women and men "friends" what they really think - and got very different answers

The results suggest large gender differences in how men and women experience opposite-sex friendships. Men were much more attracted to their female friends than vice versa. Men were also more likely than women to think that their opposite-sex friends were attracted to them - a clearly misguided belief. In fact, men's estimates of how attractive they were to their female friends had virtually nothing to do with how these women actually felt, and almost everything to do with how the men themselves felt - basically, males assumed that any romantic attraction they experienced was mutual, and were blind to the actual level of romantic interest felt by their female friends. Women, too, were blind to the mindset of their opposite-sex friends; because females generally were not attracted to their male friends, they assumed that this lack of attraction was mutual. As a result, men consistently overestimated the level of attraction felt by their female friends and women consistently underestimated the level of attraction felt by their male friends."
(Scientific American)

Here's another study:

"For those who believe that men and women really just can't be friends, a new study in the journal Evolutionary Psychology has some compelling findings. The research, conducted in Norway, found that men and women fundamentally misunderstand each other: She interprets his signals of sexual interest as friendliness. He reads her signals of friendliness as sexual interest.

The study: It may sound stereotypical, but men do have sex on the mind. Researchers at the Norwegian University of Science and Technology surveyed 308 heterosexual undergrad students between the ages of 18 and 30, asking them about their friendships, sexual attractions and experiences with misread social signals.

The result was that men commonly overperceived sexual interest from women, with the female participants saying they'd had their friendly actions misunderstood by men about 3.5 times over the past year on average. On the flip side, women reported underperceiving sexual interest from men, although markedly less so.

The research falls in line with the findings of previous studies; one from 2009, for example, found that males observed women to be more seductive, promiscuous and flirtatious (indicators of sexual interest) than females observed men to be.

Evolution may be behind men's tendency to overperceive sexual signals. The Norwegian researchers hypothesized that men overperceive sexual interest in order to minimize "errors" in choosing a mate; when it comes to natural

selection, a man's ability to reproduce is paramount, so he can't miss opportunities."
(Mic.com)

And here's another one:

"Why Men And Women Can't Be Just Friends
Men and women can theoretically be friends. But in practice, it doesn't typically last very long or end well.
Cross-sex friendships are quite new, when history is concerned. For centuries, friendship was considered something you would have with someone of the same sex. If you were a man, generally you worked around men.

Most cultures believed that there were extreme differences between men and women that made it senseless to try to bridge the gap.

Part of the problem is that defining the line between a platonic relationship and a romantic relationship is difficult. When researchers have attempted to study how cross-sex friendships happen, and what discerns them from romantic relationships, there was a serious overlap.

One study conducted in 2000 noted that most young men and young women do not feel sexual attraction for their cross-sex friends. Another study from the same year stated that half of the respondents reported having sex with a cross-sex friend. Clearly, people are confused.

According to a study published in the 2012 Journal of Social and Personal Relationships, even friendships that are confirmed to be strictly platonic are actually not really. Of the respondents, the men were significantly more likely to be sexually attracted to their cross-sex friend, and were also more likely to over-report their female friend's attraction to them.

The fact is that between the sexes, there will always be sexual tension. The line between what makes you a friend, versus what makes you a boyfriend or girlfriend is blurry and reminiscent of a Robin Thicke song. If understanding how to attract people and how to understand whether or not they are attracted to was so simple and clear, it wouldn't be a constant struggle throughout the whole of humanity.

"This does not apply to me, though," you might be thinking. "I have plenty of friends in the opposite sex." But if the statistics are true, you might be wrong. You may just think that these friends are not secretly trying to groom you as date material.

Whether you go back as far as "When Harry Met Sally" or you recently streamed "He's Just Not That Into You," cross-sex friendships do not last as long. They either turn into romantic relationships, or end when it becomes awkward. Men and women can try to be "just friends," but it's rarely a smart move."
(Mens Magazine)

TOP PRIORITY: SEX

Some of you women don't seem to understand that a man's programming never lets us forget that we're dealing with a female, a potential mate. When a guy is friendly and helpful to an attractive female, it's because there's a little voice in the back of his head that says: "Hey, you never know!"

Your guy friend may deny this if you ask him. But all guys know this to be true. For us men, sex is the most important thing in the world. Men feel about sex the way vampires feel about blood. They don't just like it, they crave it. That's why vampire stories always have strong sexual undercurrents. A vampire's hunger is simply a metaphor for a man's lust. And if a guy is paying attention to you, he wants to have sex with you.

There are only 24 hours in a day. The average man has to sleep about 8 hours. And work for 8 hours. That leaves 8 hours to run some errands, drive to and from work, eat, and have some spare time. And in that little bit of spare time, a man has to figure out how to get the one thing he likes more than anything else: sex.

So when a man has to choose whether or not he will hang out with a female and spend any time, money or attention on her, the question of whether the resources he spent will result in sex plays a very big factor. If your male "friend" chooses to spend his time and money on you, it's because he thinks there is a chance it might pay off in sex at some point. If he hangs out with you instead of with some other female, it's because he thinks you are his best bet to getting sex.

The more likely there will be sex, the more willing he is to spend his little bit of free time with you. If he thinks his chances of having sex are higher with a different female, he will spent more time, money and attention on her. That's just common sense, and using his limited resources wisely.

Still not convinced that your male "friend" wants to get in your pants? Then let's look at it from another angle:

Let's assign "fun points" on a scale from 1 to 10 to different activities, based on how much fun they are to a man. Let's say bowling is so much fun, it gets 6 fun points. And playing video games is even more fun, so it gets 7 fun points on our man scale. Having a barbeque is so much fun for a man, it gets 8 points. Going to the park and playing football with our buddies is so much fun, it gets 9 fun points. And going to a stadium and watching an NFL football game is so freakin' awesome, it gets a perfect 10 on the fun point scale.

On that scale, sex is a 15. Nothing else even comes close.

When two straight guys hang out together, we are going to do whatever we can to have the most fun together. Since we don't like to have sex with each other, sex is off the table. The next best thing we can do together to have as much fun as possible, is going to a football game, or playing video games or going bowling, or getting drunk, or something along those lines. But if given the choice, of course a man would much rather have sex with a woman, than play video games with our buddies.

If a guy "befriends" an attractive woman, the most fun

thing he can think of to do with you is to have sex. Nothing else even comes close. So when a man hangs out with a woman, having sex is the one thing he really *really* wants to do with you. Everything else is just stuff we do to get to the sex as quickly as possible.

"Nymphomaniac: a woman as obsessed with sex as an average man."
(Mignon McLaughlin)

But don't we enjoy talking to a woman? Sure, why not. Just like we enjoy talking to our buddy on our way to the football game.

If two guys love football, and we have free tickets for a game, of course we'll go see the game. Why the hell wouldn't we?

And if a man and an attractive woman are "friends" and they are in the same room together, and they have the equipment to have sex (a dick and a pussy) then why the hell wouldn't we want to make the most of that opportunity and have lots of sex? That's how a man thinks. If any of this is news to you, and you are shocked or surprised by this, it's because you're not a man, and men and women have very different sex drives.

"Women need a reason to have sex. Men just need a place."
(Billy Crystal)

Think of it this way: It's natural for a wolf to want to eat a sheep. You can train a wolf to not eat a sheep, but deep down it's unnatural for him not to eat the sheep. It goes against his basic programming. It goes against everything it means to be a wolf. If you put a wolf and a sheep in a room together, eventually the wolf will eat the sheep. If the wolf is wild and untrained, he will eat the sheep right away. If the wolf is domesticated and well-trained, he will behave himself at first, but eventually he will eat the sheep. It's just a matter of time until he has a moment of weakness.

Put a man and a woman on a deserted island, and sooner or later they will fuck. That's just how we are programmed. We all know that, even if we sometimes don't want to admit it. If a man admits to his wife that he finds his secretary attractive, it will open a whole big can of worms, because his wife is not going to be ok with the idea that her husband spends way more time at work with his hot secretary than with his wife at home. And you're certainly not going to be ok with it, if your husband and that blonde whore at work are "friends" outside of work, and they meet up after work to do things together "as friends" or they call or text each other all the time outside of work.

And of course we men are not ok with the idea that our wives or girlfriends meet other attractive men at work, because every single one of these guys could be a potential mate, and a potential competitor for our wife's attention. That's why a lot of men were against their wives joining the work force in the first place. They felt threatened. They feared it would destroy their relationship. And rightly so, as the huge increase in the number of divorces showed.

HOW CHEATING HAPPENS

Movies, TV shows, books and gossip magazines are full of these stories: A woman betrays her man with his best friend. Or a boss sleeps with his secretary. Or a college girl's best guy friend from childhood suddenly becomes more than that. Film stars who work together on a movie end up hooking up. High school students meet to study after school, and end up making out. Every porn movie and every romance novel revolves around one of these basic mating storylines. An attractive male and an attractive female meet, and they end up hooking up sooner or later. Because that's what the word attractive means. They are sexually attracted to each other. They are programmed to want to mate.

People are attracted to different things. Some men are attracted to big boobs. Some men like small perky boobs. Some men like blondes, some men like brunettes. Some women are attracted to sweaty hunks. Some women like smart nerdy guys. Some women are attracted to muscles and a huge dick. Some women like dignified older men. No matter what your preference is, when you find someone attractive for some reason, it's your ancient mating programming talking. You're judging the other person on their viability as a potential mate.

Studies have shown that being attractive has a whole lot of advantages. People treat you nicer than if you're ugly. That's because when you're attractive, more people want to mate with you. And doing nice things for you is their way of getting their foot in the door with you, just in case the opportunity to mate might present itself at some point. So when that guy at work is extra helpful, he's not just being friendly. He is pursuing you. But don't get too excited. He's doing the same thing with every other attractive female who crosses his path.

When I was younger, I used to play a lot of online games on the Xbox and Playstation. Guys treat each other like crap in those online games. We're always trying to be cocky, and there is always a lot of primal chest thumping by zit-faced wannabe alpha-males, even if it's just trash talking over the headset. But as soon as there's a female player, all the guys are suddenly extra helpful to her.

If a guy isn't very good at the game and asks other players for help over the headset, "Hey, I'm new at this game. Can someone tell me which button throws a grenade?" the responses from the other guys are usually something along the lines of: "Go fuck yourself, loser!"

But if a girl, preferably with a hot profile picture or a sexy voice, doesn't know which button to press, all the guys are outdoing each other in being helpful: "Hey sweetie, wanna join a private one-on-one game so you and I can practice the game? I'll show you where all the weapons are hidden on the map and some other cool tricks!"

The difference between scenario A and scenario B? In scenario A a guy asked for help. He's a potential competitor. In scenario B, a female asked for help. She has a pussy. That's the big difference. That makes her worth pursuing, no matter how unlikely the chance that they will ever actually meet her in real life. The probability of mating with her is not as important as the possibility, no matter how remote.

It's like playing the lottery. It doesn't matter how extremely low the chances are of winning. You gotta be in it to win it. Hitting on every girl in sight is like buying a whole lot of lottery tickets. You never know, one day one of them might actually pay off.

You women are no less interested in mating than we men are. But since you play a different role in the process, and you have different programming, you go about it a different way. Your main focus is not to spread seed but to have stability. So you tend to be less interested in having as many different sex partners as possible, and more interested in climbing the social ladder, to have a bigger and better nest for your offspring.

BACK-UP BOYFRIENDS

One way to ensure stability is redundancy. Hospitals have backup generators in case the power goes out. That's how they ensure their patients' stability. A lot of women like to do the same thing, even if you don't want to admit it. You like to have one or more back-up boyfriends in reserve, just in case things don't work out with your current boyfriend.

Nowadays, a lot of college girls tell their boyfriend "oh don't worry about him. He's like a brother to me." But more often than not she ends up hooking up with her so-called "brother" at some point, and her boyfriend was right to worry about the other guy.

You may not want to admit that your best male friend could be a potential mate for you if your current relationship falls apart. But be honest: Have you ever considered hooking up with him if all else fails and you can't find a better mate before your biological clock runs out? Sure you have.

And trust me, your husband or boyfriend is acutely aware of that fact. To us, you having a best guy friend, means you always have a back-up boyfriend, just in case. You may not see it that way, but we men do. You may not think about fucking your best guy friend right this very minute, but if our current relationship falls apart and then that other guy becomes your back-up boyfriend at some point, and you move in with him because you seek the stability of a relationship, of course sex will be involved then. That's just how the game works.

"Emotional Cheating: Are You Guilty?
Like many women, René (who asked that only her middle

name be used), a writer from northern New Jersey, had two husbands: a regular spouse and a "work husband," a man - interesting, smart, funny - with whom she spent 9 hours a day. The chemistry was obvious, but nothing ever "happened." Or did it?

They made a beeline for each other every morning, and their chats became more and more personal. "I definitely talked to him about things I didn't talk to my husband about, including my husband, because my marriage was so unhappy," René says. He sat a little too close at meetings. She admits she fantasized about a relationship.

Was she cheating? Gail Saltz, MD, associate professor of psychiatry at New York-Presbyterian Hospital/Weill Cornell School of Medicine, says "probably."

"Many of these emotional affairs do move into a sexual affair," Saltz says. "If they don't, it's easy enough to say to yourself that you're not doing anything wrong."

The problem, she says, is the attachment to this other person impacts the marriage. "Ultimately it ends painfully one way or another: Your marriage ends, or you've got to give this person up."
(Web MD)

It's not easy to find that special someone you can spend the rest of your life with. And when you have found that special person, all sorts of factors try to pull you apart again. Don't add one more strain.

WHY PEOPLE GET DIVORCED

One in two marriages end in divorce. Often because a couple doesn't notice how they slowly drift apart, because we have more in common with someone else and develop emotional intimacy with that someone else. We find some other shoulder to cry on, or we can't wait to tell that someone else about our day. And then eventually people cheat with these co-workers or friends of the opposite sex.

"Emotional affairs are very real things. In fact, over half of all emotional affairs start out innocently as online friendships. More than 70 percent of those friendships or flirtations will end up as real time affairs.

So how do you know if you are having an emotional affair? It typically starts out as a friendship, so it can be confusing to discern when things become inappropriate or unacceptable. The important thing is to determine where your friendship crosses the line. It's a slippery slope from friend to emotional affair and then to secretive sexual relationship.

Many emotional affairs start at work. Having a friend or a "cube mate" can be a lifesaver if you are working long hours in a less-than-perfect environment. It feels great to have found someone special to talk to, someone who makes you laugh and with whom you can share your day-to-day frustrations - even your hopes and dreams.

If you are telling your work friend all about your problems at home, you are asking for trouble. You're creating a unique intimacy with this person and cutting out your partner at home, essentially creating a bond with your new friend to the exclusion of your partner. Once you have established that you can talk negatively about your partner with this person, you are setting up a close and emotional relationship, as well as an opening where this person can move in to fill the needs that your partner isn't. This is a difficult question, but one you should ask yourself: are you sharing your unmet needs to subconsciously see if this person will meet them?

You are watching to see how far you can take the sexy banter. Sure, it's fun to tell dirty jokes occasionally. And yes, it might be okay to send them that sexy YouTube music video - depending on context. But think about why you are doing it. And be honest with yourself: are you testing them to gauge their reaction? Perhaps they are telling you the things you want to hear, and as such, you are now pushing the envelope to see how far things will really go. Riding the edge can be exciting, but it can also be dangerous and disrespectful to your partner.

If they start calling you in the evening, you are crossing the line. If you are texting on the weekends, you are no longer just work friends. If you find yourself waiting for those texts and those phone calls, anxiously checking your phone and responding immediately, you should refocus your attention and look honestly at the situation. You may be more emotionally involved with them at this point than with your spouse. Ask yourself: is there more to this friendship than I want to admit to my partner? Am I being honest with them and with myself?

If these three warning signs - contacting them outside of work hours, pushing the friendship edge and inappropriate sharing - are true for you, you may be having an emotional

affair."
(PsychCentral.com)

And that's why one in two marriages fail. That means your marriage has a 50% chance of falling apart. So when you feel insecure and jealous about your significant other's close opposite-sex friend, you're not being paranoid, you're being realistic. And if you have a close opposite-sex friend, you can't blame your partner for worrying that sooner or later it will break up your relationship somehow.

"So how can you recognize an emotional affair? These signs may indicate that a relationship has gone too far:
-You share personal thoughts or stories with someone of the opposite sex.
-You feel a greater emotional intimacy with him or her than you do with your spouse.
-You start comparing him or her to your spouse, and begin listing why your spouse doesn't add up.
-You long for, and look forward to, your next contact or conversation.
-You start changing your normal routine or duties to spend more time with him or her.
-You feel the need to keep conversations or activities involving him or her a secret from your spouse.
-You fantasize about spending time with, getting to know or sharing a life with him or her.
-You spend significant time alone with him or her."
(Focus on The Family)

Divorce statistics don't take into account all your other relationships that fell apart. If you dated nine men before you got married, that means your relationships so far had a 90% failure rate. And most likely meeting someone of the opposite sex (maybe when you went to college, or started a new job) and getting close with him had something to do with that. Do you really need a close intimate friend of the opposite sex that increases the odds even further that your current relationship will break apart too?

ROMANCE: A TRICK GUYS USE TO GET LAID

When a guy acts like your best friend and offers you his shoulder to cry on, so you can cry to him about your current unhappy relationship, it's because we're trying to get our foot in the door with you. We're trying to be your go-to guy. He is not trying to be a true friend and help you fix your relationship. He has an ulterior motive. He is trying to replace your current boyfriend or husband. So when you grow more and more distant from your current boyfriend and get closer and closer to your best male friend, because he seems to understand you oh-so-well, it's no coincidence. That was his plan from day one, because he never really wanted to end up in your "friend zone" to begin with.

We men know that most of you women want to have an emotional connection with someone before you sleep with him. We men know that a lot of you women think it's romantic to be friends first, and then the friendship blossoms into a relationship. Men know that we have to jump through all these hoops first, before we can get laid. And that's really all romance and courtship is to a man: hoops we have to jump through to get laid.

We men pretend to be "just a friend" at first, even though we want to sleep with you from day one. Otherwise we wouldn't be spending any time, money or attention on you, because these are limited resources and we need these resources to attract a mate. We can't afford to squander them. So we apply these resources to the female that looks to be our best bet to get laid. But we also know that we can't tell you on day one that we want to sleep with you, because you'll think it's creepy. So we play along with the illusion that it's "just a friendship" that "suddenly" developed into more, when you finally feel inclined to sleep with us "because we have a deep connection." But that was really our goal from day one.

You can do a simple test: Next time you talk to your best male friend, tell him that you feel very close to him and that you have been thinking about what it would be like to sleep with him, because you two have this deep connection. Ask him if he would be open to that. Of course he will say yes. Because that was the whole reason why he was courting and wooing you in a slow process that you mistook for "just being friends."

"A woman can become a man's friend only in the following stages: first an aquaintance, next a mistress, and only then a friend."
Anton Chekhov

HOW TO HAVE A HAPPY MARRIAGE

If you look at the history of the human species, male-female friendships outside of mating are not normal. It's a recent, modern invention that jeopardizes monogamous relationships as we know them today.

Some people talk about polyamory as the next logical step for our species. A sexual free-for-all without exclusive relationships, similar to the free love hippie movement of the 60s, where everyone is eternally single and can date as many people at the same time as they want and sleep with whoever they want, whenever they want, as if having sex with someone were no different than playing ping pong.

Call me old-fashioned, but that's not my cup of tea. I happen to like being in a monogamous relationship with my wife. That's why I keep my dick in my pants, because I know that having sex with someone else for five minutes is not worth destroying the life my wife and I have built together.

And to avoid any temptation or risk, I don't have any close female friends anymore. Sure, I have some female acquaintances, but I make sure I don't discuss intimate details with them or cry on their shoulder. Such emotional intimacy is reserved for my wife. If there's something on my mind, she's the person I talk to. She's the one I talk to about my day, or my hopes and dreams for the future. I love her, and I want her to be sure of that. I don't want her to ever feel like she's competing with some other woman for my affection or my attention.

If your current relationship is important to you, don't go out of your way to jeopardize it. Don't put strain on your relationship by having close, emotionally intimate opposite-sex friendships, even if there is no sex involved yet.

If you're not happy with your current relationship or you're not really serious, and you want to play the field and see what else is out there, then having lots of friends of the opposite sex is your best bet, because each one is a potential mate. But if you actually love your current partner and you want to build a future together, then opposite-sex friendships are toxic. That sort of thing is the #1 reason why relationships break up, because every affair first starts out as a casual opposite-sex friendship.

And that's why men and women can't be just friends.

If you enjoyed this book, you'll love:

Bad Choices Make Good Stories
The incredible true story of a teenage hacker from Germany who goes to New York, looking for love. What could possibly go wrong?

Oliver, a teenage hacker living in Germany, meets Donna online. She's an American girl living in New York. After chatting and talking on the phone for months, he finally decides to surprise her with a visit. But he soon finds out that things are not what they appeared to be, and that this visit will change his life forever.

"This generation's version of Catcher in the Rye.
I kid you not. It's that good."
★★★★★ *- Readers' Favorite*

Lightning Source UK Ltd.
Milton Keynes UK
UKHW020646210820
368607UK00014B/1372